Lean Six Sigma

Beginner's Guide to Improving Quality, Speed, and Efficiency, With the Six Sigma Methodology

Wayne Peters

© Copyright 2022 - All rights reserved.

The content contained within this book may not be reproduced, duplicated or transmitted without direct written permission from the author or the publisher.

Under no circumstances will any blame or legal responsibility be held against the publisher, or author, for any damages, reparation, or monetary loss due to the information contained within this book, either directly or indirectly.

Legal Notice:

This book is copyright protected. It is only for personal use. You cannot amend, distribute, sell, use, quote or paraphrase any part, or the content within this book, without the consent of the author or publisher.

Disclaimer Notice:

Please note the information contained within this document is for educational and entertainment purposes only. All effort has been executed to present accurate, up to date, reliable, complete information. No warranties of any kind are declared or implied. Readers acknowledge that the author is not engaged in the rendering of legal, financial, medical or professional advice. The content within this book has been derived from various sources. Please consult a licensed professional before attempting any techniques outlined in this book.

By reading this document, the reader agrees that under no circumstances is the author responsible for any losses, direct or indirect, that are incurred as a result of the use of the information contained within this document, including, but not limited to, errors, omissions, or inaccuracies.

Table of Contents

INTRODUCTION 1

CHAPTER 1: PRINCIPLES OF LEAN 7

UNDERSTANDING THE BEGINNING 7
PRINCIPLE ONE: IDENTIFY VALUE 9
PRINCIPLE TWO: MAP THE VALUE STREAM 10
   Eliminate Wasted Process: Muda 14
PRINCIPLE THREE: CREATE FLOW 20
   Unbalanced Process: Mura 20
   Kanban Boards 21
   Cumulative Process Flow Mapping 23
   Overburden: Muri 24
PRINCIPLE FOUR: ESTABLISH PULL 28
PRINCIPLE FIVE: SEEK PERFECTION 31
LEAN PRINCIPLES: SUMMARY OF LEARNING 32

CHAPTER 2: SIX SIGMA METHODOLOGY 35

SIX SIGMA VALUES 37
   Customer Focus 37
   Problem Solving 37
   Overcome Variation 38
   Clear Communication 38
   Agility 39
   Scientific Process 39
HOW TO DEFINE QUALITY 40
   Voice of the Customer 40
   Voice of the Process 44
WHAT DOES SIGMA MEAN? 47
SIGMA BELTS EXPLAINED 49
   White Belt 50
   Yellow Belt 50

Green Belt *51*
Black Belt *51*
Master Black Belt *52*
SIX SIGMA PROJECT MANAGEMENT METHODOLOGY 53
Define *54*
Measure *55*
Analyze *56*
Improve *58*
Control *59*
DECIDING WHICH PROJECT SHOULD START FIRST 60
SIX SIGMA METHODOLOGY: SUMMARY OF LEARNING 61

CHAPTER 3: LEAN SIX SIGMA IN PRACTICE 63

EXAMPLE PROJECT ONE: TVS INC.—TELEVISION CASE IMPROVEMENT 64
EXAMPLE PROJECT TWO: INSUREITNOW—CUSTOMER SERVICE
EFFICIENCY IMPROVEMENT 67
EXAMPLE PROJECT THREE: RESTAURANT 1.0—IMPROVED DISTRIBUTION
CHAINS 69
SIX SIGMA IN PRACTICE: LEARNING OUTCOMES 72

CONCLUSION 75

A SUMMARY OF LEAN AND SIX SIGMA IN COMBINATION 75
ENDLESS POSSIBILITIES FOR YOUR OWN ORGANIZATION 76

REFERENCES 79

Introduction

Whenever there is a product for a customer, there is a value stream. The challenge lies in seeing it. –Rother & Shook

Do you have rework taking up more space in your warehouse than finished goods? Have you got customer service concerns flooding your inbox? Are you struggling to keep up with the pace of incoming orders? Do you feel like your organization is sinking?

These are all common concerns for new and established companies alike. What if I told you that there is a way to start managing these concerns confidently and reduce them permanently. You can, with a quality management system that focuses on providing value to your customers by addressing these kinds of hiccups. Lean Six Sigma will address all of this, and much more. Once you start to use it, you will wonder how you ever managed before learning this famous technique.

In business, whether you work in manufacturing production, or soft services delivered to customers, you are likely already familiar with problems in providing your customer with value and satisfaction. There will be times when you already know what the root of the problem is, but you may not know where to start fixing it. Perhaps, you aren't even sure how to find the root of the problem at all, and feel totally lost.

Toyota is still the go-to example of the success that a defined, and controlled, quality management system can bring. Toyota is so synonymous with Lean that the system is also sometimes known as the Toyota Production System—TPS. It's easy to see why so many people want to emulate Toyota's methods in their own organizations. They have even been declared the most valuable car brand, worth $41.1 billion (Forbes Media LLC, 2017).

In the United States, the typical cost of poor delivery in quality management systems—QMS—can eat away up to 25% of an organization's total revenue (Miller, 2020). Implementing Lean Six Sigma methodologies in place of traditional QMS can reduce this cost to less than 5% (Pyzdek, 2003).

Other proven benefits of the Lean Six Sigma method of quality management include:

- reduced number of defects
- improved process cycle times
- increased capacity
- reduced storage costs
- improved customer satisfaction scores
- increased profit margin
- improved staff morale

In this book I will teach you how to improve your quality, efficiency, and speed of service, using the Lean Six Sigma methodology. Combining the fundamentals of Lean and Six Sigma, this book will provide a fully rounded outline that you can use in your own organization to improve overall performance. Using the five principles of Lean that were set out by Toyota—with James Womack and Daniel Jones—you can shift your focus away from fighting your problems as they arise, to identifying sustainable practices that help you reduce incidents of customer concerns in the first place. Summed up, you can shift your thinking towards getting it 'right first time'. By introducing the Six Sigma ideals to drive change, you can also strive for continuous improvement with reduced financial risk.

It can be difficult to envision how theories in research papers can help your organization in the real world. Understanding how to implement something is a whole different ball game from reading about someone else doing it. When looking for key knowledge to improve your organization, resources are often lengthy, full of jargon, and difficult to understand.

It can also be difficult to learn effective quality management systems, without passing a paywall for expensive courses. Not to mention the added cost of getting your employees up to speed on the chosen system. But, Lean Six Sigma is more than a management system for your product quality. It is an organization mindset that you can foster across your whole team, to create vast, ongoing, sustainable improvements. I believe that all organizations, regardless of size or available funds, should be able to access methodologies that will help them become more competitive by understanding quality and process.

As John Shook (2021) put it: "From a lean thinking perspective, any enterprise should have a defined value-driven purpose to which all products, processes, and value streams are directed—purpose, not "profit" necessarily, is the ultimate aim." (para. 7)

Lean outlines how you can make your process more efficient, cut out unnecessary, wasted processes, and deliver your products and services faster. Six Sigma governs how you can identify sources for potential improvement, analyze its impact on the value to your customer, and plan effectively to make changes toward a real, quantifiable difference to your process. Together they forge a methodology that spans all aspects of your organization, making it easier to identify opportunities for added value or reduced excess. They can help to solve existing problems you may already be struggling with, overall, increasing your customer satisfaction, improving your margins and adding value to your organization's purpose.

After over a decade working in manufacturing, at various levels on the career ladder—always striving to make Lean Six Sigma part of the very fabric of these organizations—I have taught many colleagues and employees how to implement these methodologies successfully. I have practiced the art of taking those theory papers and producing real-world strategies that my teams can understand, adopt, and take pride in.

Have I made mistakes? Of course. That's how we learn to do better, and part of Lean Six Sigma itself is to continually monitor the progress of implemented changes, and provide feedback on their results. It aims to experiment in a controlled environment. This way, if an idea that seemed good at trial stage, may not work in the long run without a few adjustments, you'll find that out faster. Don't miss out on creating and understanding a new value stream for your organization because you're afraid of making mistakes. When you understand the system, you'll be empowered to make continuous improvements to your organization, knowing that the methodology you are following does the groundwork to allow you to make informed choices, and reduce the risk of change.

Now, I am sharing all the knowledge I gained 'in the field' with you.

In the coming chapters I break down each part of the methodology in simple terms that can make sense in any industry. Once the basics are covered, I provide exercises designed to cement your understanding, practice necessary skills, and trigger a truly Lean mindset.

I discuss examples of how you can use your new knowledge to immediately start making tangible improvements to your own organization. I want my book to help as many of you as possible, to make your organization the best it can possibly be. Examples cover three different organization types in order for them to be relatable, regardless of the sector your organization operates in, and I use scenarios from the following fictional companies:

- manufacturing or production: manufacturing televisions—"TVs Inc."
- customer service product: insurance policy provision—"InsureItNow."
- mixed organization that manufactures and serves: a chain restaurant—"Restaurant 1.0"

Let's dive in and begin your journey, following in the footsteps of greats like Toyota, Motorola and Apple, to make your organization thrive.

Chapter 1:

Principles of Lean

Understanding the Beginning

Most traditional companies find lean nearly impossible to understand, let alone implement, because their leaders lack the "lean eyes" that come from the thinking that only occurs in someone deeply rooted in the lean fundamentals. –Byrne *et al*

The first step in making changes for your organization lies in understanding how to change the way you think about delivering your services. The 'Lean' part of Lean Six Sigma comes into effect here and should be a thought process that you apply to all areas of your organization.

Lean was born at Toyota after Kiichiro Toyoda witnessed the mass production at Ford, in the United States and saw what he believed were inefficiencies. He decided that he wanted his company to focus more on the quality and value of their cars than mass quantity. The Toyota production system was set up using the ideals that he envisioned, and the elimination of waste became one of the first principles of their practice. In effect his goal was for Toyota to do more with less. They take less time for order completion, require less raw materials for the same end outcome, and take up less floor space, so they pay less in real estate. Essentially, they have become a leaner organization.

These ideas were first coined as 'Lean' by James P. Womack, Daniel Roos, and Daniel T. Jones in 1990, after working within Toyota. Womack and Jones further refined the principles of a Lean mindset in 1996 (Lean Enterprise Institute, 2020). The five principles that they ultimately defined as key to a successful Lean operation are:

1. identify value
2. map the value stream
3. create flow
4. establish pull
5. seek perfection

This is a cyclical framework that returns to 'principle one' once you reach the end. In this way, the continuous evaluation of your organization will allow you to keep making strides towards higher value for your customers and better performance for your organization.

Now you know the cycle, what do each of these stages actually mean? Let's take a look at how each principle can be implemented.

Principle One: Identify Value

Development that creates profitable value streams must seamlessly connect and align each part of the value stream, from idea to delivery. —Shook

This principle is often forgotten but should always come first whenever you want to make improvements. It's important to understand why you are making these changes in the first place. Identifying the end goal first, ensures that all of your thinking thereafter will be done with that ideal value in mind.

What is value? Value is anything in your system, process or organization that the customer is willing to pay for. Put yourself in the mindset of your customer. Are there activities going on in your organization that they wouldn't want to pay for?

Things like reworking products from poorly performing machines, or double-handling paperwork, are common examples of lost value or waste. Be honest with yourself, there is no space here for hurt feelings when you notice unnecessary practices going on in your organization. These aren't flaws in your people or vision, but opportunities to gain value back. Ultimately, the things your customer is willing to pay for should be the only operations happening in your organization.

Principle Two: Map the Value Stream

Now that you have an understanding of what you are aiming to provide your customer, the next step is to understand how each of your processes link together, to form your organization, and provide that value.

Process is defined as: "a series of actions or operations conducting to an end

especially : a continuous operation or treatment especially in manufacture" (Merriam-Webster, 2022).

In Lean thinking, this includes actions your people take, actions performed by any machinery your organization uses, actions taken to package and deliver goods, and actions taken in administration. All of these examples count toward the culmination of actions in each process you have, and there may be multiple processes for each product or service you deliver which also need to be considered.

It must be recognized that success in one of your processes alone will not generate success as a whole. For example, a successful ordering process with an underperforming delivery process will still yield poor results, because the delivery process will not be able to keep up with demand.

Your organization's processes, across every department, should all be focused towards the same goal of providing the added value we recognized in principle one. To do this, you need to assess each area of your organization, looking at every part of your work day from the point you receive orders to the point you have fulfilled them, and been paid by the customer. Next you need to assess where each of your processes touch one another, and how those touches add or subtract from the value of their adjoining process.

If you were to compare each process to a stream, where step one is the spring water outlet, and the final step is the estuary where the river meets the ocean, the equivalent visual for the connecting processes would be a map of streams and rivers interconnecting and diverging before ultimately contributing water to the same ocean. If you now replace the water in your mind with 'value', you can see that parts of some processes would be downstream from others, and rely on their inputs. Other processes will be independent streams that meet the rest at the end goal. Understanding what the 'geography' of your organization looks like, by drawing up a value stream map of every system within it, will give you an edge in recognizing how your own processes impact each other's performance.

When starting to map out your value stream, always take part personally in collecting information, do not rely on your paperwork to give you a real reflection of what goes on in your organization. Documentation of standard processes and the time they take, often deviates from reality when left unchecked for long periods of time. The goal of value stream mapping is to gain a deeper understanding of how your organization functions as a whole, so be sure to check every stage and don't rely on other team members to feed parts of it back to you. If it makes sense to you to involve several team members to help with the project, then all of you should do this initial walk through your facility and processes together.

Start your journey at your point of service, or goods out areas. This is the part of your organization that delivers directly to your customers, and will require all preceding processes to be running effectively in order to flourish. You can then work your way 'upstream' to get a clear picture of how each activity flows into the next. If you identify a reduced or blocked flow of value, you can then trace the process back towards the beginning to find which activity or incident has caused that reduction in performance.

Always create the first map of your value stream using a pencil and paper. Trust me, you will need an eraser. When you are drawing each area of your map and connecting processes together, it is not uncommon to discover that an activity you once believed fed directly to your current position, in fact takes a detour before arriving there, or requires inputs of other streams that you now need to fit into your map when you make a closer inspection. You can always scan in a copy of your finished map, if it makes sense to your organization to keep a digital record of the work conducted, but always start by hand.

Once you have a map of your organization at its current state of operation you will be able to use this as a tool for numerous things. Start first with Lean improvements to the existing flow. After that, create a standardized or ideal value stream map that you want your staff to consistently aim towards, and look for appropriate areas to insert new products or processes effectively. Remember though, that your current state map will not always be relevant and you will need to create new ones from time to time, in order to keep up with developments in your organization.

Exercise One: Create Your Own Value Stream Map

Mapping an entire organization can take time, especially if you happen to work in a large one. However, you can practice the skill of stream mapping on a smaller scale and transfer the skills across later. So, for this exercise, follow the tips above to create a value stream map of your kitchen, assuming that the end goal is to make breakfast.

It may sound simplistic but this will let you practice assessing the streams with a Lean mindset. You may want to consider the following:

- What food and drink will your breakfast end with?
- How is your breakfast plated, and how do you get the necessary crockery in place?
- How many cooking pots or pans are needed? How long does each part take to cook?

- Are there preparatory stages before you cook? Can these be done at the same time, or do they precede each other?

- Where do you store, and how do you access the raw ingredients within your kitchen?

- How do you get the groceries into your kitchen in the first place? How do you pay for them?

- Lastly, did you forget about the process for your drink?

Once your breakfast map is complete, review it. How many times did you need to rethink the order of the steps you put on the paper? How many steps did you miss and need to go back to? Do more parts of it interconnect than you first assumed?

Try the exercise again with a different meal on another day, and see if you find it easier or harder than before. You can compare these review sessions to your first experience in mapping your organization. You'll be surprised at how similar the hurdles you encounter will be.

Eliminate Wasted Process: Muda

Waste is commonly assumed to mean wasted materials or trash, but this is a simplified and literal meaning of the word. Lean thinking identifies waste as "anything that is not contributing to creating value" (Rodriguez,

2018). You will often hear this referred to as 'Muda'—Toyota's buzz word for waste—the Japanese meaning is 'fruitlessness' or 'uselessness'. So the aim therefore is to eliminate any fruitless activities within your organization that do not yield value to you.

This methodology recognizes seven types of waste:

- Transportation—this is any time that people, products or materials are unnecessarily transported.

- Inventory—this happens when excessive inventory is kept, taking up unnecessary floor space. The value to the customer, and the organization is tied up in the stored inventory.

- Motion—this refers to any time that people or machinery move a product or material further than is necessary to achieve the process goal. This includes movement that your staff undertake to retrieve tools or raw materials they need to perform the task.

- Waiting—this happens when you have staff or machinery held up by preceding processes.

- Over-processing—this is when tasks are repeated with no additional gain, or product is over handled via rework tasks.

- Overproduction—this is seen when organizations produce more than is necessary to fill orders. They may batch produce in large quantities based on an over-optimistic sales forecast, or knowingly produce more items than an active order calls for.

- Defects—this is not only a descriptor for a faulty product, but anything that falls outside of the customer's expectations. Orders delivered outside of the lead time, or broken into two deliveries if not ready in time, would also be considered defective.

Exercise Two: Looking for Value and Waste

Let's look at an example of a process within our television manufacturer, introduced earlier, TVs Inc.

1. Orders are received via email confirmation, for 105 televisions, those emails are converted to purchase orders, which are printed and then signed for approval by senior management.

2. Those signed documents are scanned back into the computer for record keeping, photocopied and then filed away in a store room.

3. The photocopies are converted to production orders given to the production department, who adds them into a bill of materials—BOM—and standard operating procedure—SOP—pack. They make batches of 150 television cases at a time.

4. The order for the cases is planned onto a machine. Some machines make more scrap than others, so they are used as a last resort when all the others are occupied with orders already.

5. The engineers set up the machine according to the BOM. They scrap any product made while calibrating the machine.

6. Production staff run the order, following the SOP. They carry work in progress—WIP—to pallets at the other end of the workshop.

7. The utilities team takes the cases to a neighboring warehouse where they are stored until required in the assembly process.

8. At the end of machine production, the pack is signed off by a supervisor and taken to the assembly department, who add their own BOM and SOP for all internal parts that are needed.

9. The assembly department then emails the neighboring warehouse to request 105 television cases for this order.

10. At the end of production, administration staff update the stock system and file away the BOM and SOP pack.

Your task:

a. Take a look at each point above and consider where you think value is added.

b. Now consider where you think value is lost through waste? What types of waste can you see here? How can you improve on what you see?

There is no 100% correct answer to this, however, if you are viewing it with Lean thinking you might identify some of the following:

a. added value
   i. ordering via email rather than post services
   ii. paperwork is carefully kept to ensure each production run is the same
   iii. assembly operations add value to previously machined products
   iv. a digital stock record is frequently updated to avoid loss of product.

b. lost value
   i. Over-processing—duplicate copies of paperwork are made. This could be improved by keeping documents in digital format and introducing digital signatures for authorizations.
   ii. Inventory—cases are held in stores between processes. This product should be moved on to the next stage of the process when needed and not held for long periods of time.

iii. Motion—production staff need to carry WIP to the other side of the workshop. designated WIP areas should be established close to the machines to reduce time spent moving away from the machine and back again.

iv. Transportation—machined products are moved to a separate warehouse, this would require the use of forklifts at a minimum, or trucks if the neighboring space is not just across the yard. This can be improved by moving the cases directly into the assembly department.

v. Waiting—cases need to be called back from the neighboring warehouse. As with transportation, this could be improved by taking the cases directly to the assembly department.

vi. Overproduction—only making batches of 150 but allowing a customer to order 105 creates a surplus of 45 cases that are not needed. The production order should instead reflect the quantity ordered by the customer.

vii. Defects—engineers scrap product every time they set up and recalibrate the machine. From the moment good cases are produced by the machine, they should be used to fill the order, regardless of whether or not the engineering team has handed the machine off to production staff.

Principle Three: Create Flow

In lean there is a concept known as 'eliminating the three Ms', standing for *Muda*, *Mura* and *Muri*. We already covered *Muda* when we looked at eliminating waste in processes, but to achieve a successful work flow *Mura* and *Muri* must also be considered carefully.

Unbalanced Process: Mura

Mura is the Japanese word for uneven, and within Lean, it is an indicator that there is a lack of control. Your processes may be culminating in products or services that meet your standards of quality, according to the concept of a pass or fail verdict, however if there is uneasiness or unpredictability in the process then your value is reduced by a lack of control.

Sometimes unbalanced activities can be easy to spot, for example, a system that can produce 20 products an hour, and pack 30 of the same product in an hour, but can only assemble 10 of those products is uneven. It's clear that your process is being held up in a bottleneck at the assembly stage and WIP will back up in the production department while the packers are stuck waiting. Such clear cut examples are not always the case, so a tool known as a kanban board can be used to map cumulative process flow and identify bottlenecks that don't appear as obvious.

Kanban Boards

Kanban itself is a large methodology of its own, and is beyond the scope of this introduction for beginners. However, I find that this method is the most effective for identifying *Mura* before you can eliminate it. Because of this effective visualization, I recommend getting to grips with *Kanban* boards early on, even in isolation to the rest of the methodology, then continue your research after you have successfully implemented Lean thinking.

The *Kanban* board gives you a visualization of exactly how much work is in your process at any one time, and which stages it is currently at. Split your board into columns, one column for each process you have. A lot of people make the mistake of allowing their process columns to be too broad, by this I mean that they take groupings too simplistically. For example using only purchasing, production, packaging, and shipping. This won't give you an accurate representation, and would be better split out even further to purchase administration, goods in process, stock rotation, production work in progress, production finished goods, packaging, warehouse finished goods, and goods out. This takes your original four columns and drills them down to finer process separations, now you have twice as many columns and will get a more detailed representation of how flow is functioning for your organization.

Once you have established a board containing an appropriate number of columns for your organization, you need to start filling them with data. In each board, populate the number of goods you currently have at each stage. For some organizations it may be more appropriate to populate these with the number of open orders you have at each stage rather than the number of individual goods. You can use this as a daily, weekly or monthly snapshot of your progress, the number you choose will be dependent on your type of organization. You can even have it updating in real time as goods move from one process to the next, but not if it's too onerous on your team.

Exercise Three: Create a Kanban Board

Go back to the process steps listed in our previous exercise on identifying value, relating to TVs Inc. Practice putting together a kanban board using the production process covered there.

Consider which parts of the process you would drop in order to reduce waste, and how many columns you would split this example into. Once completed, review your board and identify places where you could split any of your columns to create a more detailed representation of the organization. Practice splitting a process into its most detailed sections.

Cumulative Process Flow Mapping

The snapshots from the *kanban* boards can now help to produce a cumulative flow map, using a stacked area graph to plot your data. From left to right on your x-axis, plot each snapshot cumulatively added to the previous one. Point one on the chart is equal to week one data, point two equals week one and week two's data added together, point three equals week one, two, and three's data added together, and so on.

Over time, all of your plotted area for process one will increase and your base number will continue to rise. Your other processes will be higher than process one, and create a band between the two as time goes on, this will repeat for all bands. If you have an efficiently functioning flow, then all of the bands will increase in parallel. If you notice some bands are decreasing, or fluctuating in width, then it is an indication of a flow concern. The bar that is non-conforming to the rest of your chart will identify which processes are out of sync and where you need to focus your improvement efforts. In other words, showing the *Mura* you will want to eliminate.

Overburden: Muri

Muri is the Japanese word meaning 'unreasonableness' or 'impossible', in Lean it refers to overburdening your team by placing unrealistic expectations on them. This could take the form of creating expected process times that are too tight, or setting monthly goals that are too high, even pushing too many orders through the same shift or section.

Understandably the most noticeable effect of this kind of pressure is decreased staff morale and consequently, poorer performance in your teams. But the erosion of value that overburdening can cause is more widespread. On top of decreased morale, you may start to notice increased sickness, or absence in your teams due to stress. 83% of Americans report being under stress at work and this can cost organizations up to $300 billion annually (Heckman & Milenkovic, 2019).

Staff who are forced to rush to meet an unreasonable deadline will at best make mistakes due to a lack of time for conscientiousness, and at worst they will start to cut corners in process, or suffer injuries. This will also reduce your overall quality standards and result in more failed products at your quality assurance stage. If left unchecked for too long, a presence of *Muri* in your organization can result in increased staff turnover, thus increasing your training costs, as well as more feedback of customer concerns and loss of sales.

So how do you address it? It's a complicated issue and poor staff morale can be very difficult to address once it has taken hold. Clear and honest staff communications are key. Ensure that there are effective methods for managers to communicate goals and ideals with staff, but also take care to make that communication a two-way street. Team members must feel like they are able to access management when they need to, and trust that their ideas will not be brushed off by managers who consider themselves too important, or too busy, to entertain them.

A good option to facilitate this is to set up opportunities for staff representation meetings or feedback forms. One of the most important things here is to listen to your team's feedback carefully, and go on to implement their suggestions. Be sure to consistently follow up on anything that you agree to implement for them, letting them down at this stage will amplify their unease. No one will understand the stress that your departments are under better than the teams themselves, work with them to adjust your process times to reduce burden where necessary. If you find that your capacity for orders reduces, due to the necessary changes you make, then now is also the time to consider improving capacity through extra machinery or hiring more support staff.

Communication, of course, works both ways here too, you don't just need to listen to your team but you also need to be sure that project communications, and instructions, are disseminated to departments in a timely manner. A team member will feel overburdened if they find out about changes at the last minute before a deadline, this is especially true of middle management and supervisors who take the responsibility for their team's performance. Be sure that your internal communications are clear and in a format that is accessible for your staff, so that no one is left guessing how a project should go.

Another option is to access your team's skill set, are you making the most of team members who can perform multiple roles? And, do all of the team members have the necessary training to confidently and safely conduct their duties? If the answer is no for either of these questions then it would be beneficial to put aside time for training updates.

You can also identify weakness in processes that lead to overburden by making use of your kanban boards and cumulative flow to identify bottlenecks. Often when a particular part of your process is overburdened it will result in WIP piling up for an individual team. Once you pinpoint a weakness using this method, it is important to visit the teams involved and witness an average day for them in person. This may give a clearer picture of issues cropping up for them than any paperwork could show you.

Finally, but most importantly, you can introduce the practice of *Jikoda*. *Jikoda* is a word coined by Toyota that derives from the Japanese word for 'automation'. *Jikoda* doesn't necessarily mean to 'automate' your production with robots etc., instead it aims to allow processes to be 'automatically' controlled by the people who run them. It is the most powerful tool in combating *Muri*. This concept puts power into the hands of your team to call a stop to a process that they believe is failing. If a problem occurs, they can stop production and apply a solution before continuing. This creates an instant signal that an issue needs to be addressed before it reaches the point of overburden. Additionally, it allows your team to feel like they are in control of their duties, rather than expected to carry on at all costs.

Exercise Four: the Three Ms

Choose one department of your organization, look at it in isolation from the rest of your organization for the purposes of this exercise. Make a list of the processes that occur in this department and how many team members you have acting within them.

Once you have your list, consider where this department falls, subject to the three Ms:

- Muda: Where is waste happening in your processes?

- Muri: Do you have an even distribution of WIP, are there any bottlenecks?

- Mura: Do you know how your teams are coping in this department? If you have identified a bottleneck, how does this affect them? Do they have a method by which they can escalate any issues they encounter?

Principle Four: Establish Pull

Most organizations in the West function on a 'push' model, this means that they forecast sales, and base their production on forecast alone, then push the product out the door, often via hard sales. Lean subscribes to a 'pull' method instead, this is sometimes referred to as the "just in time" method, as opposed to producing "just in case" orders materialize.

The pull method receives orders first and only produces what is needed to fill those orders without any excess stock creation. This limits waste naturally, as well as reducing risk of depreciating value on holding stock. Forecasting is still necessary to ensure your organization is prepared for demand, but call-off orders can be established from those forecasts to create pull triggered by customer demand. Call-off orders are a niche contract framework where a customer can secure large orders that are intended to fill their needs over a long period of time, and then call for that order to be filled in parts on a weekly or monthly basis through its duration. These contracts can benefit both the customer and the organization supplying the goods, by reducing the quantity of stock that either is required to hold at any one time. Additionally, the customer has reassurance that all their requirements for a project can be secured at a stable price point, before they begin. At first this may appear to be a risk for the organization providing the goods as they won't be able to fluctuate price in reflection to raw material cost. In reality, this is outweighed by a certainty that they will have incremental sales for at least the next year, in some situations these contracts can span five years or more.

Byrne (2022) refers to this as working to *Takt* time, where all process tasks are directly timed to customer demand, creating a "Sell-one Make-one" rhythm that exemplifies the ideal of Lean. *Takt* is a German word meaning "a precise interval". Toyota adapted this into the concept of *Takt* time, to represent the intervals at which production flows from one stage to another. It is a calculation that governs the rate of production. Dividing the available production time by level of customer demand, provides the length of time required for each interval in order to spread demand evenly across production availability, preventing unnecessary rush or overproduction.

Pull systems also reduce pressure on teams by allowing them to pull from the preceding process when they have capacity, rather than having WIP pushed upon them. A key part of this is to establish a system by which each team can signal that they are ready to take more work. This can be done by allowing teams to pull from preceding departments, and not allowing them to release products to down-stream departments until that department initiates pull.

Limiting the amount of WIP that can pass through your process at any one time is also important. This can include, but is not limited to, standardizing process times according to your bottlenecks, and only planning one product or model, to flow at a time, through an open channel. Studies suggest that multitasking can actually reduce efficiency, as it can take up to 15 minutes for the brain to refocus when changing tasks, whereas a dedicated approach to one flow at a time can increase productivity (Total CSR Inc., 2022).

One western organization that is a great example of a pull system is Apple. Following the return of Steve Jobs in 1997, the organization turned its fortunes around, becoming the world's most valuable brand, worth $170 billion (Forbes Media LLC, 2017). Jobs created an organizational culture that elevated customer value to the number one factor of importance, claiming that *"you've got to start with the customer experience and work back to the technology"* (Monaghan, 2020).

Exercise Five: Looking for Examples of Pull

You know now that Lean originated within Toyota, and that Apple adapted a pull strategy to improve their performance in the 1990s. These two companies are giants in their respective fields, but can you see examples of pull systems working in other places?

Take a look at the leading companies in your own industry, who are they? Do they generate hype around their products whenever they launch something new like Apple does? Do they have a brilliant reputation for customer service like Toyota? Put aside some time to consider how big, multinational brands in other industries conduct their business, can you see if they are also following this system? Lastly, look at smaller scale things around you, what daily activities only draw value from something when it is needed? Once you become confident in identifying where pull works successfully, you will be empowered to start thinking of ways to implement it in your own organization.

Principle Five: Seek Perfection

Perfection is defined as: 'The quality or state of being perfect... an unsurpassable degree of accuracy or excellence" (Merriam-Webster 2022).

It could be construed as foolish to assume that you have reached perfection. Toyota accepts that true perfection is an ideology rather than an end goal. They believe that continuous improvement is always possible. An organization successfully operating within Lean thinking will understand that added value can always be found in fine-tuning their process. Through continued efforts to return to the principles of Lean which capture your organizations value streams and flow efficiency, it is possible to guide the evolution of your organization over time. Re-capturing a visual of your current state at regular intervals can reveal opportunities for improvement that may have been hidden beneath more pressing concerns at the time of your first review.

The aim is to repeatedly refine your organization, and to look for opportunities to deliver value to your customers with less waste, and more efficiency than before. This is a part of Lean that managers often fail to implement. They view an exercise in Lean as a one time project that will improve their organization and be easily maintained. This isn't the case, for Lean to function at its best within your organization it needs to be a way of thinking that is adopted by team members at all levels. It is a way of thinking that empowers every person that touches a process with the ability to call attention to areas that they believe can be improved, at any level.

This is where Lean thinking and Six Sigma project management collide to become the methodology of Lean Six Sigma. Implementing the tools of Six Sigma, to continually revisit how you view your organization is key to seeking perfection over time.

Lean Principles: Summary of Learning

In this chapter we learned that Lean was developed within Toyota as a methodology to put the customer first, and develop an organization that drives customer value by reducing waste.

The five key principles of Lean are: identify value, map the value stream, create flow, establish pull, and seek perfection.

You completed exercises which encouraged you to develop a Lean mindset when viewing your organization and the world around you. Now you should be comfortable with the following skills before progressing to chapter two:

- understanding a process at all levels
- drawing a value stream map
- recognizing where value is added or subtracted
- identifying types of waste, and where they can be removed from your value streams
- taking a snapshot of your organization by creating a kanban board
- identifying the three Ms in your organization, and developing ways to start eliminating them
- recognizing what a pull management system looks like

Chapter 2:

Six Sigma Methodology

Six Sigma benefits others besides customers. When operations become more cost-effective and the product design cycle shortens, owners or investors benefit too. When employees become more productive their pay can be increased. Six Sigma's broad scope means that it provides benefits to all stakeholders in the organization. –Pyzdek

Six Sigma is a quality management system that demands that the highest level of quality be delivered, from all processes, to the customer. Like Lean, its end goal is to eliminate *Muda*, however, Six Sigma's main difference compared to Lean thinking, is that it is highly targeted and relies on proven statistical methods to facilitate change.

Six Sigma has three main target areas of its projects: customer value, stakeholder value, and team wellbeing. It was developed within Motorola in the 1980s, following a change in management in the United States, from American to Japanese team members. The change resulted in a decrease in the number of production defects to 1/20th the previous standard (Pyzdek, 2003). It forced Motorola to recognize that it had a serious quality problem that needed to be fixed, and resulted in the development of Six Sigma in response to increasing customer demand, along with increasing complexity of modern processes, which leads to more potential for problems to arise.

The methodology seeks to put in place a dedicated team whose sole goal is to recognize opportunities for improvement, or identify areas of concern, and drive change internally. As a methodology, it focuses heavily on continually improving processes, which is why it fits so perfectly into the fifth principle of Lean—seek perfection. For the success of the Six Sigma methodology, organizations need to do the groundwork in establishing these teams before starting individual projects for improvement.

This is a proactive approach to dealing with concerns, whereas traditionally managed non-sigma companies are more reactive. Often waiting until they see a decrease in sales, unmanageable quantities of customer complaints, or even a dropping share price, before triggering a problem solving process. The largest problem with the traditional approach is that the necessary change will need to happen regardless of the management method chosen. Leaving it until it is conducted as a response to an outwardly visible negative effect, results in the change being forced upon the organization, and rushed through, without time for the necessary analysis first. Six Sigma combats this by recognizing concerns and strategically planning an organizational change to address the affected process internally, before it spirals to have larger consequences for the organization. It can also be used to minimize risk associated with launching new products, and smoothly integrate changing customer demands.

Six Sigma Values

Like Lean has its principles, the Six Sigma methodology has a list of values which it relies on to drive the culture of an organization. These principles include:

Customer Focus

All Six Sigma projects should start with the customer in mind. All changes and projects aim to increase value for the customer as their primary objective. After the customer needs are understood, the sigma teams can work backwards up the value stream to identify parts of the process that can be altered to deliver this objective.

Problem Solving

Lean aims to deliver an everyday culture that can become part of the organization's own principles or ethos. Six Sigma, instead, focuses on solving problems. The methodology seeks to identify areas of variation that create unbalanced flow within processes. An organization should actively seek to remove any obstacles to improving its value streams, to allow the sigma team to be the most effective that it can be.

Overcome Variation

Six Sigma focuses on process variation, it considers that variation to be the number one cause of *Muda*. All sigma projects will take form once a variation is discovered, this could be highlighted by a customer concern, internal team member, or found in regular monitoring of process data. Whatever the source of variance, returning a process to Six Sigma becomes the secondary objective of any projects, after customer value.

Clear Communication

All team members involved in Six Sigma projects need to have received clear instructions on the project goals. It is essential for project managers to communicate, in as many channels as possible, the reasons for change and the ideals pursued by the organization. Team members who are comfortable with the old ways will be resistant to change. Their concerns can be overcome by presenting the benefits of the new way.

Team members aren't the only ones who need to be kept in the loop. Customers should also be given transparency whenever a process change affects the products they purchase regularly. Managers must celebrate the improvements with them, and manage their expectations for the potential scope of any upgrades or modernization.

Agility

The focus on reducing variance increases the level of predictability for each process. In turn, this allows orders to be planned more accurately for the time needed and materials used, during production. This increased accuracy gives an organization more control and flexibility in their offerings. The organization can respond to increased order demand, or change in customer need, more effectively. Becoming more agile gives the organization an edge over competitors, they can provide added value, or new products, more quickly but still with a high degree of confidence in product quality.

Scientific Process

All Six Sigma projects are based on scientific principles. The idea of a shift in variance of process is essential to how every project is managed. Each stage of a Six Sigma project is navigated methodically, and in the same order. There are numerous tools available to analyze its ongoing performance. The overall goal of this principle is to reduce risk to the organization by ensuring that change is managed effectively, reducing guess work, and specifically targeting problem areas in each process.

How to Define Quality

Six Sigma combines two types of quality control to account for naturally occurring variations in an organization's process: acceptable quality levels defined by your customer, and internal acceptable levels of quality geared towards minimizing loss. These two areas are known as: The voice of the customer—VoC—, and the voice of the process—VoP.

Voice of the Customer

When deciding how to define and control your quality levels, you first need to start with your customer's expectation, this is your VoC. Traditionally, the perceived customer expectations have been used, in quality control, to set a "gold standard" product or service, that you would provide them, in an ideal world, with no issues. There is a limit to how far you can drift from this standard, before the customer decides that your product is no longer of value, or is unsuitable for use.

The gold standard is known as the nominal value. The limits at which a product becomes non-conforming to that standard are known as your lower specification limit—LSL—(equal to your nominal value minus the downward variance) and your upper specification limit—USL—(your nominal value plus the acceptable upward variance).

To put this into context, let's look at our manufacturer TVs Inc. When TVs Inc. produces a television case for a 52" television, it should measure 52" diagonally across the opening for the screen. The customer can accept the opening being as narrow as 51.75" before the screen will no longer fit into place, and as wide as 52.25" before the gap around the screen will be too large. In this example, the LSL will become 51.75", the nominal value is 52", and the USL will become 52.25". Anything produced that is either smaller than the LSL or larger than the USL would be considered a defect.

Using the LSL and USL described for TVs Inc. above, the plot of distribution for a batch of 1000 television cases is detailed in the table below, and produces the distribution curve in the following chart.

Screen Opening Size (Inches)	Number of Instances (Batch of 1000)
51	1
51.25	11
51.5	35
51.75	98
52	714
52.25	97
52.5	34

Screen Opening Size (Inches)	Number of Instances (Batch of 1000)
52.75	9
53	1

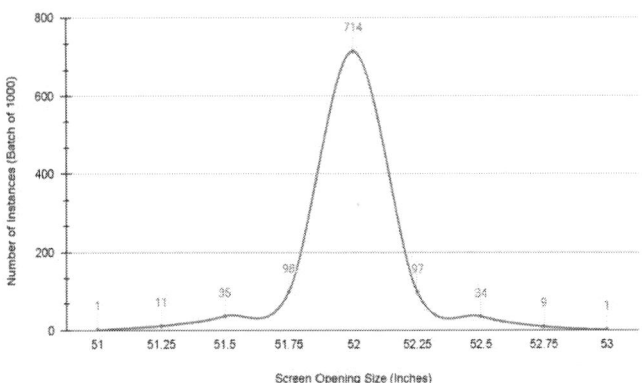

When TVs Inc. collect data from their process over the course of a week and plot it into a distribution chart, with the *x*-axis representing screen opening length, and the *y*-axis representing the number of times that size was produced. They find that the distribution curve of the spread in sizes produced, follows the shape of a bell curve. The further away from ideal that a product becomes, the less instances of that defect size are found. This is a common variance in data, and the narrower the peak found when plotting distribution, the less variance from the nominal value is present in a process. You may see this kind of distribution referred to as an average distribution curve.

Putting this distribution in the context of the VoC, any parts produced that fall outside of the LSL and USL, can be seen at the lowest points of the curve either side of the distribution chart. By presenting production data in this way, managers can gain a clear picture of the process performance. If a distribution chart highlights a peak that isn't central, or near central, then it indicates that too many of the products manufactured are falling outside of your customer's acceptable limits, and your process needs to be analyzed to find areas of concern. Likewise, a very short peak, a curve that appears more like a mild wave shape than a bell, also indicates that a process is creating too much waste.

Exercise Six: Creating a Bell Curve

Choose one production run, or order, to collect data from one of your processes. Collect a set of at least 100 data points to ensure that you get a fair representative curve, but don't overburden yourself by choosing to tackle a whole week or month's worth of data if you produce hundreds of thousands of items a day.

Use the data you have collected to produce your own distribution chart for your selected process.

Once you have your curve, mark your chart with your own LSL and USL, this will show you how many instances of defects are currently present according to your customers requirements. You now also know the effect of the VoC on your process.

Voice of the Process

The VoP model of quality makes two assumptions: firstly, that every process will experience a natural amount of variation, even when tightly controlled, and secondly, that after a product leaves your organization, a customer is likely to find extra defects that have not previously been identified. In response to these assumptions, this model aims to use the natural variation in a process to redefine internal process standards, and minimize the risk of defects being present post production. It does this by defining how much variation is acceptable on either side of the nominal value before a process becomes unviable. In this method, 'unviable' means a process that is displaying a high level of variance from its nominal value and has become unpredictable. That unpredictability then leads to a number of negative effects:

- excess use or loss of raw materials
- increased production time
- increased product defects at point of production
- increased labor required for rework
- increased customer concerns

- decreased customer value, and faith in the organization
- decreased sales

This method addresses these concerns by identifying where the average—mean—value for the product specification lies, and then adjusting the process until the mean accurately falls within the LSL and USL. A mean is calculated by summing the total value, and dividing it by the number of data points present. If a mean is not equal to the nominal value set by the customer, or less than 1.5 units value away from it, then it is an indication that a process is not operating as efficiently as it should be. For our TVs Inc. example, the unit value is 0.25" since the measurements are recorded in quarter inch increments. The unit value will be defined by the process that is being measured, if your organization does not manufacture, this could be the number of days taken for a service to be delivered, and the unit value would be one day. For the healthcare industry you could be measuring how many patients are moved through a department each day, and the unit value therefore would be one patient.

Considering the unit value, for TVs Inc. the mean would be calculated as: the total sum of all the screen openings measured, divided by 1000 products in the batch. Using the data we already have, the mean calculation looks like this:

Screen Opening Size (Inches)	Number of Instances (Batch of 1000)	Sum of Openings Measured at Each Value (Inches)
51	1	51 x 1 = 51
51.25	11	51.25 x 11 = 563.75
51.5	35	51.5 x 35 = 1,802.5
51.75	98	51.75 x 98 = 5,071.5
52	714	52 x 714 = 37,128
52.25	97	52.25 x 97 = 5,068.25
52.5	34	52.5 x 34 = 1,785
52.75	9	52.75 x 9 = 474.75
53	1	53 x 1 = 53
Sum of All Openings Measured per Batch (Inches)		51,997.75

51,997.75/1000 = 51.99

Therefore the mean of this process is 51.99".

This would identify that for TVs Inc. their process is functioning so that their average production is extremely close to their desired nominal value, and so it is performing within specification limits more often than not. Using the VoP alone, this would be considered a properly functioning process.

Exercise Seven: What is Your Mean?

Using the data that you collected for exercise six, calculate the mean value for your chosen process. Is your mean close to your nominal value? If not, is its variation acceptable to you, or do you see that an improvement is needed?

What Does Sigma Mean?

After defining quality, the next step is to decide upon a standard level of acceptable variance, which both minimizes loss, and increases value. This is achieved with the understanding, and application of, "standard deviation" represented as a sigma level.

Here is the part of the methodology from which Six Sigma derives its name. Sigma is a reference to a letter from the Greek alphabet 'σ'. In mathematical processes sigma represents 'deviation', which in terms of quality management is the variance in value of a process between its maximum potential and a range of non-conformance.

Traditional non-sigma quality management methods often use a range of acceptable non-conforming activities or products, expressed as a percentage, and representing a sigma level of three or four. Historically, the use of percentages was useful, however, modern processes contain many more steps, and therefore, more opportunities for a defect to occur within a single process.

Six Sigma defines its range of variance as a figure of parts per million—ppm—produced, instead. The standard acceptable variance for sigma level six is 3.4 ppm, this is a ten fold improvement in the number of defects present in a process using traditional percentage based metrics. By implementing this standardized acceptable variance, Motorola tripled their profits to $498 million in 1989, and reached sales of more than $16 billion by 1993 (Pederson, 2000).

Sigma level three is equivalent to a 93.3% quality pass rate, and level four represents 99.3% pass rate. Based on the old standards of quality management, this seems respectable, but if we equate this to how many parts, in a million opportunities to pass, become defects, it can be between 6,210 and 66,800 defects per million products produced (Brenig-Jones & Morgan, 2012). This level does not account for any natural shift in the mean of a process, it relies on defined LSL and USL that are tightly confined at the edges of acceptable quality measurement.

Sigma level six however, creates a drastic improvement on these figures. By aiming for 3.4 defects per million, this increases the quality pass rate to 99.99966% or an amazing 0.00034 defects per every 100 opportunities (Brenig-Jones & Morgan, 2012). Organizations operating with Six Sigma therefore have a reduction in waste and an increase in production efficiency compared with non-sigma quality management methodologies. Instead of allowing a process to define their LSL and USL at the edges of acceptable quality, they actively seek to improve a process until it reaches sigma level six. This accounts for a shift in mean of 1.5 deviation points and widens the range of the LSL and USL to account for this shift.

Sigma Belts Explained

There are other statistical measurements and tools, beyond those I have mentioned, that can be of enormous value when reviewing your processes. These may be dependent on your specific industry and are too numerous to cover here. These tools can require a deeper knowledge of math on the part of the manager undertaking the review. Because of this, Six Sigma organizations often implement qualification belts to structure their quality improvement teams. Training courses will frequently use these belts to advertise the depth to which they teach the subject of Six Sigma.

White Belt

The white belt is not a recognized qualification, but instead it refers to team members who do not have any authority or control in defined projects. You will still want to communicate to these team members the basic aims and principles of sigma, in order to achieve a cohesive staff understanding of your change management and quality methodologies. As with Lean, it is important that every member of the organization understands and takes part in a culture of continuous improvement.

Yellow Belt

Though this is the first recognized qualification level, many companies skip directly to green belt training when looking to upskill their team members. I don't recommend this strategy, as in my experience, failing to train yellow belts will leave a skill gap in your projects. These team members should be chosen from frontline process staff and are the ones who have the deepest understanding of how an organization functions on a day to day basis. It is imperative that you at least develop an internal training system for yellow belt proficiency, otherwise projects will suffer from a lack of practical input.

Yellow belts are people who do not have authority to create projects or lead teams, instead doing the physical work of running trials and providing feedback. They are machine operators, customer service agents, facilities staff etc. Yellow belts are the grassroots of an organization who will hold full time positions in service or production, only being freed up to assist the sigma project teams when necessary. They are the team members that project leaders will rely on to implement changes and record data. They must be fully trained in any operations covered by their designated role, and know the basics of a sigma project flow. They must be empowered to raise concerns identified in the course of their daily activities.

Green Belt

Green belts are data handlers and project leads. They may function in any role across an organization, but part of their daily activities will be dedicated to driving Six Sigma projects. It's common to see green belts working on two or three projects at a time within their own departments. They have a sound understanding of the core methodologies of Six Sigma, will be able to analyze data, identify areas for improvement, coach yellow belts on project goals, and make basic decisions to direct projects that they lead.

Black Belt

Black belts are members of a sigma team who are wholly dedicated to either quality improvement or change management within an organization. They are management team members, experienced project managers who lead green belts, and drive change towards variance reduction. Black belts may also be responsible for financial budgets and will typically oversee five or six projects at a time. Black belts must have a cross-departmental understanding of the organization to ensure that projects cover all necessary process streams.

Master Black Belt

Master black belts are seasoned professionals, they have the authority to facilitate major change. They are sometimes referred to as project sponsors, and are responsible for the overall quality management, and cost of quality budgeting for the organization.

These team members must be given full freedom to implement large projects and organization-wide changes in ethos. They are dedicated to leading, and coaching all of the other sigma team members, and are usually senior management, or board members. Clear communication of quality goals is key to their success.

Exercise Eight: Looking for Your Sigma Team

Take a look at your organization's structure, find suitable team members to work on your sigma projects. Consider how many green and black belts you would need to structure a successful project team of your own.

Is your organization able to implement one green belt per department? Would it be more appropriate to nominate a small handful of people who can perform projects across adjoining departments? Create a hierarchy of your ideal team to visualize what your Six Sigma could look like if fully integrated. To determine where to start, look for at least one member of upper management or directorate that can take on black belt training. If you can't spare a manager full time, can you hire a new manager dedicated to your Six Sigma team? Nominate at least two members of staff who can become green belts and run smaller projects. Once you have this core team in place, you can expand the team over time to a suitable size for your own organization.

Six Sigma Project Management Methodology

Now we know what sigma means, and where to start facilitating your own sigma team. How do they start their projects? Six Sigma methodology uses two project management flows: DMAIC—define, measure, analyze, improve, control, and DMADV—define, measure, analyze, design, verify.

DMAIC is used to continuously improve existing processes and can be considered as a cyclical process. DMADV is used to design and implement new products or processes. Lean Six Sigma as a quality control methodology only uses the DMAIC system, as such, this is the one that I will cover here.

Define

The first stage seeks to define the scope of any project before it starts. The project managers will need to understand who the project is for and why they are undertaking it. The ultimate goals of a project should always be defined at the start and referred to regularly throughout the process to remind team members what direction their focus should be concentrated on. The following things need to be considered:

- Who is the customer that this project serves?
- What is the business case for implementing this project?
- What do you want the project to deliver for your customer?
- What is the current state of the process value stream map?
- What is the problem you are seeking to rectify?
- What is the project goal? How will it deliver results?
- What is your deadline for this project?

A common mistake at this stage is to assume what a customer needs rather than to discuss their expectations with them or respond to a concern they have already expressed. Sometimes improvement projects are not triggered by the customer, but they must still be focused on delivering added value to the customer. Be sure that internal projects are defined carefully to avoid losing focus.

Measure

This stage is all about understanding how your process is measured, and therefore, how the results of your projects can be measured. Consider whether there is enough data currently available to understand the current key performance indicators—KPIs. Now is also the time to check that any KPIs you already have in place are measuring an appropriate value. This is the point at which the green belts will access the mean performance and sigma value, to have a baseline against which you can measure success. It is important to ensure that any measurements you choose can be collected over time and will present data which captures a process flow, not just a snapshot. Things to consider in the measurement stage include:

- Is current data available?
- Is existing data accurate?
- Do you need to measure a new metric?
- If data isn't reliable, how will you collect the missing information?
- Does the KPI reflect the aim of the project?

Ways to assess whether the measurements taken from a process are actually providing value to the project team can include:

- checking that the metric used to measure will give real time information on a process without needing to be converted or otherwise manipulated before it makes sense in the context of the objectives.

- checking that the data makes sense to everyone involved on the project, if some data is too complex for those actioning changes, it needs to be reviewed again.

- checking that your data points are numerous enough to show a trend in process over time.

- checking that the metric chosen reflects the needs of the customer, so that the project team can be sure they are making changes that are positively affecting the value to the customer.

Analyze

The analyze stage seeks to understand performance, and identify areas that can be improved to meet the goals set out in the define stage. If a process is not functioning at its best, then this stage also takes into consideration how the organization can allocate resources to make necessary changes. Things that should be outlined:

- How can the identified process be improved?
- Who would implement it?
- What obstacles would stop the improvement efforts?
- Can obstacles be removed entirely or reduced?
- What resources will be needed to make the proposed changes?
- What would failure look like? How will this be avoided?
- Is the proposed change viable as a solution?

During the analyze stage, high level managers or directors will sometimes need to approve budgets for the projects to continue. This is especially true if the potential solution involves purchasing new equipment, relocating premises or hiring new staff. These solutions can be costly, but shouldn't be overlooked. There are situations where the resulting value of an implementation will outweigh the initial cost very quickly. Every organization will have their own time limits in which they would expect to see added value before they approve improvement measures. In my own experience, three years is a good benchmark for large or expensive projects to start producing returns.

Improve

The improve stage sets out to do what it says on the tin, metaphorically speaking. Its focus lies in making improvements to the process, based on all of the information gathered in the previous stages. This is the point where a project team may conduct trials on suggested changes, or start to make long term changes if the risk of going ahead without trial is minimal. The sigma project team should focus on how their changes affect the process, and what value they will gain from the actions taken. It's important to consider the following aspects before physically implementing changes:

- What steps are needed to adopt the change?
- How are the changes focused on achieving added value?
- What will the value stream look like with the new changes in place?

For larger projects, carefully plan the improve stage before making any changes other than a trial or experiment for data collection purposes. Develop ideas for how information will be collected throughout the process change, to ensure adequate feedback on process trends.

Control

The final stage of DMAIC is to control progress and ensure that any gains in value are sustainable. Consider how you are going to keep the team within budget, how it will reach its goals and how you will pull things back if it starts to waiver. Additionally, it's the stage where paperwork will be put in place to standardize the new process in the future. Things to consider are:

- What metrics will be used to continue monitoring performance in future?
- Who will take ownership of the process after the project ends?
- How will gains be monitored for ongoing consistency?

This stage is often missed or not thoroughly thought out in project management. The control stage is crucial to success, it keeps team members in check, continually refocusing efforts on the defined objectives. It is also the stage at which feedback will be collected. This feedback must be taken seriously and used to tweak ongoing project improvements until the Six Sigma team is certain that results are repeatable, consistent, and within the scope of the measurements and objectives.

Deciding Which Project Should Start First

One sticking point for many organizations is making decisions on which projects should be targeted first, especially when there may be limited finances to employ large sigma teams. Sometimes, priorities are easy to access, as urgent matters present themselves with large financial losses or critical failings in customer service. As with other quality management concepts it isn't always obvious where the root of the fault lies, this is when the application of decision making tools reduces risk of incorrectly allocating resources in problem solving.

There are many tools that can be used by sigma teams, including tree, fishbone, and affinity diagrams, which are already used in traditional quality management systems. I recommend getting to grips with creating matrix diagrams, they provide a quantitative representation of the weight that each problem holds in regards to the value they add or detract from your customer, and they are easy to communicate to staff.

Matrix diagrams allocate a score, between one and five, to each concern in relation to the customer's needs. These problems are then charted against the causes of each concern, essentially visualizing the 'what', and 'how' of concerns. The number of occurrences for each concern type at each cause are noted. Occurrences are then multiplied by the customer score for the concern type, and totaled by cause, to give an overall score. The problem with the highest score is considered most important to be actioned first. The same matrix diagram also gives you an indication of where your second and third project focus should lie, but it is still good practice to revisit this problem solving tool at the start of each round of organizational improvement activities.

Six Sigma Methodology: Summary of Learning

In this chapter we learned that the Six Sigma methodology was developed within Motarola in response to increasing customer needs and a demand for continued modernization of their organization. We looked at how defining quality is the first step in controlling improvements consistently and with reduced risk. VoC and VoP were discussed and the importance of implementing a Six Sigma team that makes use of the hierarchy of 'belt' qualifications.

The five key values of Six Sigma are: customer focus, problem solving, overcoming variation, clear communication, agility, and scientific process.

The Six Sigma project methodology used in Lean Six Sigma is the DMAIC system.

You completed exercises which encouraged you to learn how to determine if your own processes are functioning healthily, using data distribution charts, and you looked at how you could place project teams within your organization. You should now be comfortable with the following skills before jumping into Lean Six Sigma across your organization:

- understanding the core values of Six Sigma
- defining quality with confidence
- understanding LSL and USL
- drawing a distribution chart for your processes
- interpreting a distribution chart to visualize the effectiveness of a process
- understanding how a Six Sigma team should function within an organization
- using the stages of DMAIC appropriately

Chapter 3:

Lean Six Sigma in Practice

As lean thinking continues to spread to every country in the world, leaders are also adapting the tools and principles beyond manufacturing, to logistics and distribution, services, retail, healthcare, construction, maintenance, and even government. –
Lean Enterprise Institute

Now that we have covered the theory behind Lean and Six Sigma, and practiced some of the skills required, this chapter will take you through some project examples in our three fictional companies: TVs Inc, InsureItNow, and Restaurant 1.0.

The intention of these project examples is to show you what these theories might look like in practice, and how they can be flexible enough to fit multiple organizations or industry types. These examples are not intended to break down every single step of Lean Six Sigma, but instead they seek to provide an overview, at a high level, of how projects for improvement may progress in different situations. In every project, different stages will show themselves as key markers for success in that particular project, or points at which an "Ah-hah" breakthrough moment is reached.

We have already talked about TVs Inc. and used them as the main focus for Lean Six Sigma in manufacturing. This is because the methodologies were developed in the manufacturing industry and that is where the principles were tested. As such the first project example here will also focus on TVs Inc. However, if you work in a soft service industry, such as finance, health care provision, or marketing, or for an organization that spans more than one industry type, then you may wish to skip to the next examples.

Example Project One: TVs Inc.—Television Case Improvement

TVs Inc. have identified waste generated in the production of the television cases, requiring many hours of rework on each batch before screens can be fitted, the cost of producing cases has increased sharply in the last year. They have also received several complaints from their customers about the quality of the cases they receive. There is an increased number of televisions that have an unsightly gap around the screens, raising concerns. As a result, the management team has decided to investigate and launch a project to improve the situation.

The first stage for TVs Inc. is to review their Lean principles to ensure that they are appropriate for the process: identify value, map the value stream, create flow, establish pull, and seek perfection. Managers select team members from each stage of the process, walk the entire chain from distribution back to raw materials and find that there are a number of steps on the paperwork for the value stream that are no longer being actioned. Engineers are no longer running products, to create an acceptable quality case, before handing it to production. During production the machine cycle time varies widely and is dependent on production staff opening the machine to remove the product. It is believed that this variance is leading to misshapen screen openings and requiring cases to be reworked before they can be passed to the assembly stage of production. It is clear that their flow is disrupted, and staff are feeling pressured to rework cases, to get them out as quickly as they were before rework was necessary.

Following their review of the process, management decides to hold retraining for engineers, to ensure that machines are not handed to production before an acceptable quality part has been produced. For the varying cycle time however, there does not appear to be an immediate fix, so the Six Sigma team is asked to investigate further.

The Six Sigma team then follows DMAIC methodology to resolve the variance in production of the television cases. The project is initially given to a green belt who conducts the define, measure, and analyze stages. They identify that the most appropriate solution is to introduce a robot arm to remove parts from the machine, to standardize cycle time and remove the variance added by human interaction with the machine. Since this solution would require an investment of capital they take it to the black belt for further advice.

The black belt reviews the stages that the green belt has conducted and agrees with their suggestion. They work on a report outlining potential costs and benefits of adopting the robot solution, then champion the project to management and the team of directors, who will be able to make an informed decision on whether or not to invest, based on the reports provided.

The team of directors approve the project and the black belt coaches the green belt to find potential suppliers for the robot. They develop trial ideas together and the black belt uses a budget, defined at project approval stage, to engage a supplier in trials. Through these trials, the black and green belts work together on the improve stage, and then a robot is purchased. The black belt then takes a step back and allows the green belt to continue the control stage, to monitor the success of improvement and put in place the necessary paperwork to include the robot in the new standardized process. Finally, they report back to management that the project has been successful, based on a new cycle time variance within Six Sigma deviation and the elimination of rework entirely. The project has achieved its goals by resolving the immediate quality problem, it has added value to the customer by removing instances of non-conforming product, and reducing cost of the process to the organization by eliminating the labor used in rework.

Example Project Two: InsureItNow—Customer Service Efficiency Improvement

InsureItNow has experienced a reduction in the number of customers choosing to renew their policies in the last six months. The team of directors is concerned about the loss of revenue and have directed the management team to investigate the issue.

The management team chooses to use department representatives for an open discussion about why they believe customers are no longer renewing. These team members speak with customers on a daily basis and the management team wants to get insights from that experience. The team reports that customers often complain about the amount of time they are left on hold, and the automated telephone system often directs them to a dead end. This prompts the managers to look at the value stream of the customer service process. Upon requesting data from their customer service team, they discover that a large percentage of customers that hang up during an attempted customer service call do not renew their policies. This then prompts management to ask the Six Sigma team to find a solution to the problems with the telephone system.

The green belt defines the objectives as: add value to customers by making the telephone system easier to interact with, reducing the number of customers that choose to abandon their call attempt, and increasing sales of policy renewals. As per Six Sigma values, the customer-focused objective becomes the primary goal. There is currently no data for customer satisfaction in the customer service process, so during the measure phase a new KPI is created to gauge the level of customer satisfaction, alongside the call time data they already have. Whenever a customer calls in, they receive a survey via SMS, to assess their satisfaction with the service they received.

Once data becomes reliable and one months worth of customer interactions with the customer service team are analyzed, the Six Sigma team decides that the most appropriate solution to the issue is to work with the telephone technicians to change the automated system, reducing the number of options that a customer can choose and shortening the length of the introductory messages to each part of the automated menu. The green belts are able to implement trials for the automated system with the help of the technicians. They don't require further authorization due to the limited risk. They also make a suggestion to black belts and management, that an additional two customer service operatives working on each shift would reduce hold time for customers by providing enough capacity to serve an extra 48 callers per day—based on two eight hour shifts daily and an average successful call length of 20 minutes, which they propose, follows the trend illustrated by data collected the previous month.

The black belts compile a report on the cost of implementing new team members against the cost of lost renewal revenue and present the report to the team of directors. With all the information at hand the directors approve the additional headcount for the customer services team, they approve a round of hiring and interviews to start the following month. The project then returns to the green belt who enters the control stage, defining new paperwork and helping managers to compile new training for staff that is aligned with the messages provided to customers via the new automated telephone menu.

After six months, the project is closed by the management team who consider it to have been a success. Data provided by the Six Sigma team shows that average length of time on hold, and total call length is reduced, customer satisfaction surveys are consistently returning higher scores, and the rate of policy renewal has doubled.

Example Project Three: Restaurant 1.0—Improved Distribution Chains

Restaurant 1.0 notices an increasing number of their chain restaurants reporting difficulties keeping desserts well stocked and a resulting decrease in up-sales to customers coming in for a meal. Sales figures don't seem to suggest a particular problem with desserts, as they have sold in the same quantities each month over the last year. As a result the Six Sigma team is immediately asked to investigate and find a solution.

The team interviews managers of the restaurants that are complaining of stock problems and discover that they have been running out of stock before the end of the week. They don't believe that there is a sales or quality issue with the desserts but they often get told by the production facility that they can't supply them with the requested quantity of product. Based on these interviews the Six Sigma team decides that the issue must be originating in the production facility and turn their focus there instead.

They walk through the value stream for the process of dessert production, starting at the distribution facility and moving backwards. The process matches the written standards throughout production. However, a problem is identified in distribution where product builds up in the freezers and isn't loaded onto trucks despite the necessary stock being available for orders. This triggers the Six Sigma team to start a project that aims to improve the efficiency of dessert distribution between the manufacturing facility and the chain restaurants.

The entire project is handled by green belts who define the goals of the project as: Increase dessert sales by providing more opportunity for the customer to buy when there is a demand for desserts, and reduce the amount of stock that builds up in the freezers by improving delivery of goods to their restaurants.

They measure progress by the number of desserts delivered and subsequently sold by each restaurant in a week. While collecting data, the Six Sigma team discovers a recurring issue where the distribution company is unable to send full size refrigerated trucks to the production facility as contracted. In their place half of the vehicles sent are refrigerated vans, which can carry significantly less stock, but no allowance is made for the missing capacity.

The Six Sigma team works with their procurement team to renegotiate the terms of the distribution contract, and request that only higher capacity tracks get sent for their refrigerated collections. The distribution company agrees to allocate extra capacity to Restaurant 1.0's orders and have a new timetable put in place by the end of the month.

Following the update to the distribution contract, the Six Sigma team continues to monitor delivery quantities and sales of desserts in the restaurants that were affected by previous capacity issues. After three months, data shows that dessert sales have increased by 20% and the managers who previously complained about their stock issues report no more problems. The warehouse team also reports that the freezers are now holding the product for less time before it can be distributed. The project is considered a success and closed.

Exercise Nine: Seeing DMAIC Across Project Types

For each of the example projects above, create a list of which actions or outcomes represent each of the define, measure, analyze, improve, and control stages. You may find it useful to create a table with one column for each project stage, and populate the contents with the ideas from each example that you feel represents it. Although some stages will feature more prominently than others in the examples, you will find that all of them follow the Six Sigma project methodology.

Next, think about which of these companies' operations closest fit the kind of service that your own organization provides. Build from that to think about your own management structure, and how a project may look across your own departments. Compare this to the spread of staff that you identified for training in exercise eight. Did you identify enough people to sufficiently carry out a variety of future projects?

Six Sigma in Practice: Learning Outcomes

In this chapter we saw examples of how the Six Sigma DMAIC methodology looks in the context of different industry sectors. You practiced identifying the five stages in different scenarios across these project examples, and considered how they relate to your own organization. You now have the knowledge to understand the following concepts in practice:

- Lean Six Sigma methodology is adaptable across multiple industries.
- Soft service industries are not excluded from using Lean Six Sigma.
- Different belt levels in a sigma team add value via their respective roles, but do not work in isolation from one another.
- Practices that are contracted externally can also be a focus of improvement.
- Budgets can be individually defined per project, but also amended based on the outcome of initial research carried out by the sigma project team.

Conclusion

A Summary of Lean and Six Sigma in Combination

Customers want to emotionally engage with a brand, make their decision to buy with the right information and execute their decision with as little friction as possible. –Monaghan

The goals of the combined Lean Six Sigma methodology are to put the customer at the center of all activities intended to improve processes. By focusing on increasing the value to the customer at each stage, an organization can continually strive for high levels of quality, process efficiency, and increased speed of order fulfillment.

Lean principles can be used to implement a culture that permeates your whole organization and inspires all team members regardless of role, to take an active part in ensuring that production is done right the first time. It empowers them to draw attention to concerns that they believe can be addressed to improve the value stream.

Once Lean is in place and an organization is happy with the level of quality control that it gives them, they can then turn to Six Sigma in order to fulfill the final principle of Lean—seek perfection. Proactive problem solving within an organization reduces risk of process failure, increases customer confidence, and allows quick reactions to demands on their product offering. Lean Six Sigma continually provides a basis of values and principles that the management team can return to time and time again, in order to find solutions to organizational problems and reduce their process variation.

If an organization ever notices that its quality management systems are slipping away from their ideal, the fundamentals can be reviewed and new Six Sigma team members trained to provide a fresh view on the processes in place.

Endless Possibilities for Your Own Organization

The 'Gemba' is a Japanese term for the 'actual place'—that is, where the action is. Only in the Gemba can you truly see how things are done and it's the only place where real improvement can occur. You may be able to draw up new ways of doing the work in some central management location, or in an engineering office, but the reality is the Gemba. That's where things are defined, and refined, to produce genuine and effective change. –Brenig-Jones & Morgan

Welcome to the world of quality measured by ppm, achieving your organizational goals through a customer focused approach, and scientifically backed decision making that drives your projects to success. I'm excited to think of all the possibilities that my book has opened up for you. These methodologies can be adapted and applied to virtually any industry and situation. I challenge you now, to visit your process areas, get familiar with the nitty gritty of how your organization functions, and implement these methodologies to turn your organization into the best possible version of itself.

I have provided you with all the basics needed to start improving your organization today. With these tools and the skills you have practiced throughout this book, you will be able to confidently advocate for a Lean mindset to process control. You will also understand how careful and defined project management methodologies, in this case the DMAIC system from Six Sigma, can be sewn into the fabric of an organization and create reliable continuous improvement to the level of value that your organization can offer to your customer.

You have read about how these methodologies have had incredible results for global industry leaders like Toyota, Motorola, and Apple. I have shown how you can replicate their ideologies to improve your own quality management systems. You now have an impressive list of understanding and skills that will allow you to make a start on improving your own organizations efficiency and quality right away. Use the information you have gained here to champion the implementation of a structured Six Sigma team, or make informed choices for your own departments, on nominating team members for further training in the green and black belts.

References

Aartsengel, A. v., & Kurtoglu, S. (2013). *Handbook on Continuous Improvement Transformation: The Lean Six Sigma Framework and Systematic Methodology for Implementation*. Springer Berlin Heidelberg.

Brenig-Jones, M., & Morgan, J. (2012). *Lean Six Sigma For Dummies*. Wiley.

Byrne, A., Ethington, E., & Zayko, M. (2022, January 26). *Ask Art: Why Are the Four Lean Fundamentals So Important for Making a Conversion to Lean?*. Lean Enterprise Institute. https://www.lean.org/the-lean-post/articles/ask-art-why-are-the-four-lean-fundamentals-so-important-for-making-a-conversion-to-lean/

Forbes Media LLC. (2017, May). The World's Most Valuable Brands 2017. Forbes. https://www.forbes.com/pictures/591c87fc31358e03e5593101/8-toyota/?sh=1c7603fb4518

Heckman, W., & Milenkovic, M. (2019, September 25). *42 Worrying Workplace Stress Statistics*. The American Institute of Stress. https://www.stress.org/42-worrying-workplace-stress-statistics

Kanbanize. (2022). *What Is Value in Lean?*. Kanbanize. https://kanbanize.com/lean-management/value-waste/what-is-value-lean

Kooijman, S. (2020). *What is the connection between Lean and Toyota?*. Lean Six Sigma Group. https://leansixsigmagroup.co.uk/lean-toyota/

Lean Enterprise Institute. (2020). *A Brief History of Lean*. Lean Enterprise Institute. https://www.lean.org/explore-lean/a-brief-history-of-lean/

Merriam-Webster, Incorporated. (2022, April 5). *Perfection Definition & Meaning*. Merriam-Webster. https://www.merriam-webster.com/dictionary/perfection

Merriam-Webster, Incorporated. (2022, April 11). *Process Definition & Meaning*. Merriam-Webster. https://www.merriam-webster.com/dictionary/process

Miller, K. (2020, June 2). *Evaluating the Cost of Quality: It's Simple Math*. IQVIA. https://www.iqvia.com/locations/united-states/blogs/2020/06/evaluating-the-cost-of-quality-it-is-simple-math

Monaghan, S. (2020, August 22). *Design For Demand. Shortly after his return to Apple… | by Steve Monaghan*. Medium.

https://medium.com/@steve.monaghan/design-for-demand-1c27a4be4716

Pederson, J. P. (Ed.). (2000). *International Directory of Company Histories*. St. James Press.

The Performance Institute. (2021, April 30). *Six Sigma Belts - Definition, Levels, Roles and Training*. The Performance Institute. https://www.performanceinstitute.org/blog/six-sigma-belts

Pyzdek, T. (2003). *The Six Sigma handbook: a complete guide for green belts, black belts, and managers at all levels*. Mcgraw-hill.

Rodriguez, T. S. (2018, June 19). *LEAN Production: the method that made Toyota the most valuable car brand in the World*. Medium. https://medium.com/drill/lean-production-the-method-that-made-toyota-the-most-valuable-car-brand-in-the-world-13279db0b224

Rother, M., & Shook, J. (2003). *Learning to See: Value Stream Mapping to Add Value and Eliminate Muda (1.3 ed.)*. Taylor & Francis.

Shook, J. (2021, August 4). *Create Profitable Value Streams*. Lean Enterprise Institute. https://www.lean.org/the-lean-post/articles/create-profitable-value-streams/

Smalley, A., & Kato, I. (2017). *Toyota Kaizen Methods: Six Steps to Improvement*. Taylor & Francis.

Smith, B. (n.d.). *Six Sigma Belts – What is the Difference?*. Six Sigma Online. https://www.sixsigmaonline.org/six-sigma-belts-what-is-the-difference/

Total CSR Inc. (2022). *How Multitasking is Killing Efficiency And 3 Tips to Avoid It*. Total CSR. https://totalcsr.com/resource-center/how-multitasking-is-killing-efficiency-and-3-tips-to-avoid-it/

Visco, D. (2017). *5S Made Easy: A Step-by-Step Guide to Implementing and Sustaining Your 5S Program*. Taylor & Francis.

Printed in Dunstable, United Kingdom